# LOOKING

# FOR

# A FUTURE

## Abdulatif Adem

# Imprint

1st edition, 2023

© 2023 Abdulatif Adem

Proofreading: Daniel Kaempfer
Produced and published by: BoD – Books on Demand, Norderstedt
ISBN: 978-3-7578-8083-5

« Everyone has a dream, some make the first step to achieve their dream, and may encounter difficulties along the way, these difficulties make them more haunting to realize their dream. And others have not yet dared to take their first step. The first may be successful and can reach their goals. And the others still have the chance to take their first step».

**Abdulatif Adem**

# Chapter One

# Abdul and His Grandmother

One day, 13-year-old Abdul was with his grandmother. She told him stories from her childhood. When she finished her first story for him, she wanted to start telling a second story. Something came to Abdul's mind and he said to his grandmother

"I want to emigrate to Sudan."

The grandmother was surprised at what she heard from her grandson. She answered him:

"What are you saying, boy, are you crazy? Do you know how dangerous this thing is? Never think about it. And don't tell your family what you told me. Because they won't accept anything like that from you."

Abdul was silent for a bit at first and then said to her: "Why not, grandma? Where is my brother?".

He meant his brother, who had been arrested six months before by the army of the Eritrean dictatorship and up to then nobody had heard from him.

"My fate will also be like the fate of my brother and his friends. There are no good schools in this country, no universities, there is no freedom. How can anyone have a good future, grandma? The people of this country are still finding themselves between the living and the dead. No one will sleep well as long as this unjust power stands," said Abdul with a sad face.

The grandmother was touched by what she heard from her grandson and said:

"It's okay, my child. I understand what you're saying. Let me think a little about this topic. Tomorrow we'll talk about this it. It's lunchtime now. Go have lunch with your brothers."

Abdul went and ate his lunch, he then went back to his grandmother and asked her: "Grandma, have you thought about it?"

"Didn't I say, I'll tell you tomorrow?" his grandmother said.

"Ok," Abdul said, shook his head and left.

Abdul did not tell his family what he had spoken to his grandmother. Because his grandmother told him not to tell anyone. That day he wondered what his grandmother would say to him the following day, would she agree or say no? The next day came. Early in the morning Abdul went to his grandmother who lived near their house. He came to her and asked her:

"What are you thinking, grandma? Tell me?"

"This decision is very dangerous. But what you said is true, Abdul, no one has a future in this country. But I am very worried about you. What might you encounter on the way?" asked his grandmother.

Abdul pointed to the sky with his hand and said to his grandmother:

"Don't worry grandmother. God will be with me because God will not further oppress an oppressed person anymore".

"What you say is true, little one. God is with the oppressed," said the grandmother. And added:

"I also decided to come with you to my daughter who lives in a small village near the Eritrean-Sudanese border. We will also stay there for a few days to make sure the road is good."

"Dear Grandma, that's a great idea," said Abdul and was delighted.

The grandmother didn't want to tell his family about it. Rather, she would tell them that she was taking her grandson to visit her daughter, who lived near the border. They would also stay with her for a few days.

The grandmother told her grandson that they would leave next Sunday, which was only two days later. Abdul was very motivated and kissed his grandmother's head. The grandmother informed Abdul's mother that she wanted to take her grandson to visit her daughter, who lived near the border. And they would stay with their daughter for a few days. Abdul's mother agreed because Abdul had accompanied his grandmother on almost every visit. Abdul prepared for this trip and gathered his clothes and other items that he needed for his journey.

It was Sunday and that morning Abdul began his flight to Sudan, accompanied by his grandmother, who accompanied him to the Eritrean-Sudan border. Abdul said goodbye to his family and told them that he would come back with his grandmother in a few days. He went with his grandmother to the bus station, which was about a 20-minute walk from their home. They came to the bus station in Keren, the town where Abdul lived with his family, and took a bus to Tesseney. Tesseney is another town not far from the Sudanese border.

They boarded the bus bound for Tesseney after buying the tickets for 70 Eritrean nakfa per person. It was a long way from Keren to Tesseney. The bus started moving at seven in the morning. On the way to Tesseney, Abdul kept asking his grandmother, "Haven't we arrived yet?"

"Not yet" replied the grandmother over and over again.

Five hours into the journey, as they approached the town of Tesseney, there was a regular Army checkpoint. When they reached the checkpoint, the bus stopped and two army soldiers got on and began asking passengers for their IDs. One of them came to Abdul's grandmother. He asked her for her ID and she gave it to the soldier. He looked at the ID and handed it back. Then the soldier asked Abdul for his ID. Abdul said nothing because he had no ID.

The soldier again: "Give me your ID, boy!". He was louder this time.

"I don't have any ID," Abdul said in an anxious voice.

The grandmother intervened and said to the soldier: "This is my grandson, leave him alone".

The soldier ordered Abdul and his grandmother to get off the bus and ordered the bus driver to continue his way.

Another soldier came to Abdul and his grandmother and asked them, "Where are you going?"

"I'm going to my daughter who lives near the border. She's very sick and there's nobody next to me who could help her. We wanted to visit her and help her. As you can see, I'm an elderly woman. I can't travel alone. I can't see well. So, I took my grandson to help me with many things. I can't do anything without him, so please! Let us go," the grandmother said to the soldier.

The soldier went to his colleague, they talked for a while, then he came back to Abdul and his grandmother and said to them: "All right, you can go".

The grandmother thanked the soldier. And when another bus came to the checkpoint, Abdul got on the bus with his grandmother and they drove off to the town. After 10 minutes they reached the town of Tesseney. In the city, they treated themselves to a break in one of the cafes. After that, they went in search of a bus that went to the city of Omhajer near Sudan.

# Chapter Two

## **The Old Friend**

Abdul and his grandmother found a bus going to Omhajer. Near the bus in the bus station, Abdul saw someone he knew from their town of Keren. This person was a 22-year-old soldier. Abdul went to him and said: "Saleh!"

The soldier, whose name was Saleh, was surprised to see Abdul and said, "Abdul, what are you doing here?"

They hugged and shook hands.

"This is my grandmother," said Abdul.

Saleh also shook grandmother's hand and said,

"Hello".

They all sat next to the bus. Abdul told Saleh his story and told him that he was on his way to Sudan and that his grandmother insisted on accompanying him to her daughter, who lives in a small village near the Sudanese border. Saleh was silent for a while and smiled, then he said,

"Well, then I would have found someone to accompany me."

Abdul was surprised by what he heard from Saleh.

"Are you going to Sudan too?" Abdul asked.

"There is no other choice, I've had enough of this country. In the end I decided to emigrate," Saleh replied.

Abdul was very happy because he would not be alone on the way to Sudan. He would even have someone to accompany him. Saleh asked Abdul not to bother his grandmother and she could go home. And she should never worry about her grandson. Saleh would be with her grandson in any situation until they safely entered Sudan.

Abdul went to his grandmother who was sitting next to them. And he told her as Saleh advised him. She should never worry about her grandson, and he told her that they would go to her daughter first.

"I'll talk to Saleh myself," said the grandmother.

She went to Saleh and they talked for a while, then she went back to Abdul and said:

"Well, little one, I'll go back home. Saleh will take care of you."

"I can take care of myself too," said Abdul.

Then grandmother said with sadness in her face:

"Your mother will kill me if I go back to her without you, but don't worry, I'll make it."

Then she hugged her grandson and said to him:

"Goodbye, kid, I know you're a smart person and you'll take good care of yourself. God bless you."

Abdul and Saleh got on the bus. Abdul left his grandmother while she waved her hand at him from the window. The sadness was clearly visible in her face.

On the bus, Saleh said to Abdul, "We shouldn't sit next to each other because if we did, the soldiers at the checkpoints might suspect that we're fleeing from this country."

There were two army checkpoints between the towns of Tesseney and Omhajer. Abdul sat in the back of the bus and Saleh sat in the front. The bus reached the first checkpoint, stopped - and so did Abdul's heart. The doors opened and two soldiers got in the bus. Abdul was terrified and prayed that no one would ask for his ID. The soldiers began asking the passengers for their IDs one by one. They asked Saleh, he gave them his ID because he had a valid military ID. The soldiers questioned all the passengers who were on the bus, and then they got off without asking Abdul. Abdul was very surprised why the soldiers didn't ask him. He thought maybe because of his young age. But he was very happy because he had passed the first checkpoint without any problems. About an hour after they had passed the first checkpoint, the bus would reach the second checkpoint. Abdul was looking for a way to bypass the second checkpoint. He didn't want to rely on luck like the first time. A woman sat next to Abdul. This woman had two large bags. Abdul told the woman his story and told her that he was very scared. He then asked her to cover him with her bags as he hid under the seats when the bus reached the checkpoint. The woman was very nice and understood exactly why young people are fleeing from the country. She agreed to do Abdul this favor.

When they reached the second checkpoint, Abdul got down under the seats and the woman covered him with her bags as they had discussed. The bus doors opened, a soldier got on and told the passengers to have their identity cards ready.

The soldier got off the bus after he had finished checking and ordered the driver to proceed. Luckily for Abdul, the soldier didn't notice anyone hiding on the bus. The bus moved on and the woman told Abdul that the soldiers had left. Abdul came out from under the seat and thanked the woman who had been so nice to him. The bus that Abdul and his friend Saleh were travelling in arrived at the city of Omhajer in the evening. They got off the bus and Saleh said to Abdul:

"It's too late and dark now, we have to spend the night in this city, we have no other choice."

They went looking for a hotel for the night. They arrived at a hotel, a receptionist greeted them and then asked for their identity. Saleh had no problem because he had valid ID. But that wasn't a good question for Abdul, who didn't have any ID. They told the receptionist that Abdul had no ID and was just a young student.

"If young or old. ID card is required here. No one is allowed to stay in hotels in Omhajer without a valid ID, that's what the law says. Not far from here is a police station. You can go there, they will give you a paper after they investigate the little one. If he got this paper, he could stay at this hotel or any other hotel in town. I can show you to the police station if you want," the receptionist told them.

"No, no, it's okay, thanks, we can go alone, don't bother yourself," said Abdul and Saleh

However, they did not go to the police station, fearing that the investigation would trick them into telling the truth and then lead to prison or torture. They decided to go to the outskirts where it was quieter. They could sleep there under a tree or whatever they could find. After they got to one of the outskirts of town, they found an old hut that nobody lived in. They entered it and found nothing inside and decided to spend the night there.

"Your grandmother told me about her daughter who lives near the Sudanese border," Saleh told Abdul. "She gave me directions to her village of Qaria* (*name changed). We will walk there tomorrow. It is very dangerous to go to this village by bus. The military controls all means of transport everywhere."

"Good, Saleh, may God be with us. I will sleep now. Good night," Abdul replied.

"Yes, good night, Abdul," Saleh said.

The next day, before sunrise, Saleh woke Abdul and told him, "We have to go now."

Abdul ate his egg-filled bread given to him by his grandmother and set off with Saleh to the village of Qaria. They didn't walk on the public road because they were afraid the soldiers would see them. They wandered on side roads that led past farms. After walking for about two hours, Abdul's face showed signs of fatigue. Abdul asked Saleh to stop and take a break. They stopped under some trees that lined the whole way. Unlike Abdul, Saleh showed no signs of fatigue, but there was tension in his face as well.

"What's the matter with you? Why are you so tense?" Abdul asked.

"We got lost." I don't know where we are. But our orientation is in the opposite direction of sunrise. If we're lucky, we might get to the damn' village," Saleh replied.

"Did you say if we're lucky? What do you mean? "What if we're not lucky? Will we die?" Abdul asked again.

"If we're not lucky, we'll fall into the hands of the soldiers, but don't worry, they won't kill us, maybe they'll leave us in prison for the next twenty or thirty years, no more," Saleh said, smiling.

"No longer?"

"I'll be a young man in my thirties or at most forty when we get out of prison. But you'll be so old that you'll need a stick to lean on," said Abdul and laughed.

"Enough joking. Let's be optimistic, and God willing, nothing bad will happen to us. Now let's go that way," Saleh said, pointing his finger in a direction.

After about an hour they realized that they were lost in the woods and between the many farms. Suddenly they heard someone say to them: "Stop!"

At that moment Abdul and his friend Saleh got goosebumps. They turned around and saw an old man pointing his stick at them and saying, "What are you doing on my farm? Did you come here to steal something?"

"Finally, thank God, we found someone to show us the way to this village," Saleh replied.

"Listen. Haji, we weren't here to steal anything from you, I swear to God. We want to go to a small village called Qaria. We have got lost. And this is my little brother Abdul. We're going to my aunt who lives in that village. We heard that she is very sick, and we are coming to help her, so please, Haji, help us and show us the way," Saleh added.

A look of emotion and sadness appeared on this man's face.

"Qaria is a village far from here. Maybe an hour and a half to two hours on foot. However, I'm not asking you why you didn't go there by bus. I know that the government and the military are tough on the people and go ahead with the controls. I don't like this government and I'm not afraid of them," said the old man.

The man gave Abdul and Saleh water to drink. He walked with them on the way for a while as they were talking to each other. After a while the man stopped and said:

"Here's my limit. I have to get back to my farm to water it."

He described Abdul and Saleh the way to the village.

"God bless you and your brother. Take good care of your little brother, he is the future of this beautiful country," he told Saleh.

The kind old man didn't know that this future wanted to escape this beautiful country and emigrate.

# Chapter Three

## **Aunt Aisha**

Saleh and Abdul set out on the way the old man had described to them. After a long journey along dried up trees, in the heat of the sun at a temperature of over 40°C, they reached the village. When they reached the market of this village, they entered a restaurant. They were famished. After filling their bellies and drinking tea, they asked for the address of Abdul's aunt, whose name was Aisha. The people of Qaria village were very nice and helpful. They helped Abdul and Saleh find Aisha's house. Aisha was very surprised when she saw her nephew Abdul in front of her door. She knew Abdul well because she sometimes visited her mother and sister in the town of Keren. Aisha had five children. Two of them lived in Sudan, where they emigrated like many other young Eritreans. And three of Aisha's children were small and lived with their mother in this village, where they attended elementary school and tended goats in their spare time. Aisha's husband was a soldier. He was not present at the time. He was in some military camp in southern Eritrea.

Aisha welcomed Abdul and his friend Saleh into her home and provided them with food and water. Saleh and Abdul told Aisha that they wanted to flee to Sudan. Aisha wasn't surprised by the news as she knew it the moment she first saw them outside her door.

"I know you are fleeing to Sudan. I know you didn't come just to visit me in a village so far away that has nothing to offer," Aisha said, smiling.

But Aisha was very nervous. She feared Saleh and Abdul would be arrested at her house and the government would accuse her of trying to help people emigrate illegally.

Abdul told his aunt his story of how his way had been full of dangers and how he had come to this village with Saleh.

"Thank God, nothing happened to you," said Aisha. "Does your family know where you are now, Abdul? Does my sister even know that you are emigrating to Sudan? " she asked Abdul.

Abdul hesitated and then said, "Yes, of course, my family knows everything. My mother told me to come to you and you would help me. My grandmother even came to Tesseney with me. She would have come here if I hadn't met my friend Saleh Wouldn't I, Saleh?", Abdul added, asking Saleh for confirmation.

"What he says about his grandmother is true. And as for the rest, I don't know anything," Saleh replied.

There was no internet or any other means of communication for Aisha to contact Abdul's mother and to discover his lie that her mother was the one who had arranged for his departure. Aisha had no choice but to believe Abdul and help him. Because she knew, too, that there was no future for young people in this country. That's why her two children had emigrated to Sudan.

"I have no choice but to help you and put you up in my house. You are my sister's son, Abdul. But your mother will kill me if something bad happens to you," Aisha said.

"Don't worry, aunt, nothing will happen to me, I'm a strong person. And Saleh is with me. I trust him very well," Abdul replied to his aunt.

Aisha told Abdul and Saleh to wait five days until next Sunday. Because Sunday was the official holiday in Eritrea. Also the day of the big market in the border town of Omhajer. On this day, the

Eritrean army's control of the Eritrean-Sudanese border is relaxed, as many members of the army have Sunday off or go shopping at the Omhajer market. Aisha also wanted Abdul and Saleh to stay in their home for the remaining five days because she did not want to risk her children's lives and her own if Abdul and Saleh were arrested in that village.

Abdul and his friend Saleh stayed at Aisha's house during those five days. They waited for Sunday to begin their perilous border crossing into Sudan. The five days were very difficult and boring for Abdul and his friend Saleh. They stayed in Aisha's house all day, and some nights they walked around the village secretly and with extreme caution. During the day they sometimes played with Aisha's children. They told them stories from their lives. And Abdul sometimes helped them with their homework. The children and Aisha enjoyed the moments spent with Abdul and Saleh. Abdul and Saleh also enjoyed themselves because their worries were alleviated as they sat and played with Aisha's children.

Days passed, day by day, until the promised Sunday came. That morning, Saleh and Abdul ate their breakfast that Aisha had prepared for them. Then they dressed like shepherds so as not to arouse suspicion and so people would think they were from the outskirts of this place famous for its shepherds and many farms.

Abdul said goodbye to his aunt Aisha and her children. They thanked her for her generosity and hospitality. Signs of tension filled Aisha's face as she seemed very worried about her nephew. She and her children were sad to say goodbye to Abdul and Saleh with whom they had shared very funny and happy times. After the sad farewell to Aisha and her three children, Abdul and Saleh packed up their things and set off across the border. Saleh had acquired

*I fled from my homeland with my own freedom,*
*Where violence and injustice feel fear,*
*In another country we go to live,*
*Because injustice is scary,*
*We've come the long way,*
*With hope we go in a different direction,*
*But the way contains difficulties,*
*And caution is required everywhere,*
*And patience to achieve protection,*
*Until we get our freedom.*

~ Chat GPT

road tracking experience while serving in the Eritrean Army. Saleh walked the thorn-strewn path in front and Abdul behind him towards the village called Hamdayit, which is directly on Sudanese territory after crossing the border. Saleh, who served in the army, was a strong person who could endure many hardships and pains. Abdul, unlike Saleh, kept wanting to stop to get a little rest.

The weather was very hot. Luckily, Saleh and Abdul had brought enough water with them for their journey. After a while on the road, Abdul began to suffer from the heat, which exceeded 45 degrees Celsius. And from the giant thorns that pierced his shoes and made his feet swell and bleed profusely. Abdul tried to endure the pain in his feet and continued walking with Saleh in the scorching heat of the sun. Saleh had a good pair of sturdy shoes that the army had given him, unlike Abdul who had bought his shoes at the market in the city of Omhajer. It was a shoe that wasn't quite as stiff as Saleh's shoe. Abdul and Saleh would stop from time to time to take a little break and remove thorns from Abdul's legs that were causing him so much pain. The further they walked, the hotter the weather got. So they needed more breaks to stop and rest while walking under trees and over the thorns that lined the path.

As they walked on, Saleh suddenly saw a person with a camel sitting under a tree not far away. Apparently, the tree shaded him and his camel.

"Down, down, there's a soldier in front of us, apparently he's guarding the borders," Saleh said in a low voice to Abdul.

"Damn it, what are we going to do now?" Abdul asked.

"We have to find another way to get around the soldier," Saleh replied.

"But that would be a long way and I can't take it. I have no strength left," said Abdul. "Let's go this way, and when the soldier sees us, we're two people and he's just one person. We'll manage."

"What are you talking about? Are you crazy? Didn't you see the Kalashnikov next to him?" Saleh asked. "He has a gun, you idiot. And you, you can hardly walk. How are we going to manage that? Tell me, Rambo. Let's turn back now before he sees us," he added.

Abdul noted that tiredness and exhaustion made him say things that were not easy for Saleh, who had military experience. They took the other route and luckily, they were able to avoid the soldier with his camel. Abdul and Saleh continued their way in their exhaustion and suffering. After a while, a web antenna appeared in the distance in front of them.

"Look, Abdul," Saleh said, pointing to the antenna. "This antenna must be in Hamdayit Sudanese territory. What a day. Let's go Abdul, we're almost there."

Joy began to appear clearly on Saleh's face. Abdul was very exhausted and could hardly speak. As they approached the village, they brushed out the dust from their clothes that covered them.

"We will now enter the outskirts of the village. So we have to speak Arabic to each other so that people think we are Sudanese. Otherwise, they could inform the police. The police would arrest us," Saleh told Abdul.

In Sudan, Arabic is the country's official language. Along with the Tigrinya and Tigre languages, Arabic is also considered one of the official languages of the country of Eritrea. Abdul and Saleh had learned Arabic in elementary school, so they spoke the language well.

They came to the outskirts of the city and found a shepherd there. Saleh asked him if this village was Hamdayit. He wanted to make sure they had arrived at the right place. When the shepherd told them that this was Hamdayit, Saleh and Abdul were reassured. And they knew that they had reached their destination, their desired place.

# Chapter Four

# **Lost in Sudan**

After Saleh and Abdul had arrived in Sudan, they separated and went in different directions. Abdul went to a town called Kassala in eastern Sudan. And Saleh went to another city called Al-Qadarif. Abdul stayed in Kassala for nearly four months with his grandmother's brother and his wife, who had accompanied him to the town of Tesseney. Abdul's feet recovered from the effects of the thorns and swelling in the first few weeks.

Four months later, Abdul moved to another city. Abdul moved back and forth between Sudanese cities, including the capital, Khartoum. During his stay in Sudan, Abdul worked in different places and in different jobs. Once he sold vegetables and fruit in Kassala. And once he bought a billiards place for gambling and worked there. He even worked for the Sudanese Red Crescent with a fake certificate as a database specialist. He worked there for six months entering data on a computer until he was caught by the police and taken to a refugee camp. Shortly after entering the camp, he hid in a large truck and fled the camp. After that he continued to move from one city to another and from one profession to another.

Abdul lived in Sudan for two years and three months. During this time in Sudan, he found some of the freedom he had longed for. But he thought that building his future in this country is also very difficult, if not impossible. Abdul had heard that many young Eritreans in Sudan took a different route, a much more dangerous route than before: another migration across the Sahara into Libya, then across the sea to Italy. This idea kept haunting him until it became the subject of his discussion with the people. Abdul always heard that so-and-so got lucky and arrived in Europe and lived happily there. Or from others who were not lucky, they died in the desert or drowned in the sea. Abdul thought a lot about this theme.

One day a friend he knew in Sudan called him on Facebook from Sweden. During a long conversation with his friend, whose name was Nassir, some of them recalled the beautiful memories they had together in Sudan. Abdul told Nassir that he wanted to emigrate to Europe and that he was very desperate to leave this country. He wanted to build his future in Europe. Nassir encouraged Abdul and supported his ideas.

"I know, Abdul, that the path is very dangerous, the desert and then the sea. It's like gambling. Either you succeed and reach your goal, or you go to heaven," Nassir said to Abdul. "I know the conditions in Sudan. You know I was there. What a hard life."

"And believe me my friend, I know the situation is very serious but I see no other choice," he added over the phone.

After this conversation, Abdul was convinced that he should follow the path of his friend Nassir and flee to Libya and then to Europe. After Abdul had made his decision that he was going to emigrate, he started collecting the amount of money for the trip that he had saved from his various jobs. He then looked for smugglers who could smuggle him across the Sahara to the Libyan capital of Tripoli.

After a few days of searching, he found two people smuggling people across the desert into Libya for $1,500 each. The amount Abdul had saved was only $1100. He told these smugglers that that was all he had of the money. And that he had nothing but that. The two smugglers refused to accept anything less than $1,500. They told Abdul to bring the full amount or they would not take him anywhere. Abdul didn't have the amount he was asked for. He didn't know where to get the rest of the money from. Abdul went back to the smuggler and told them he had his phone, which was worth around $150. Abdul told them he was willing to give them the phone in addition to the $1100.

"If you accept my offer and take my phone on top of the $1100, we will have a deal. And if you don't accept it, I will look for other brokers. I will surely come up with a better offer," Abdul said to the two smugglers.

The smugglers were initially reluctant, but eventually agreed to accept Abdul's offer. Apparently there was a competition between the smugglers. So they didn't want to let Abdul go to other people. Abdul agreed with these two persons on the place and time of the journey. The smugglers told him to get to the meeting point on time, which was two days after they met. And he should bring the amount and the phone or his amount, otherwise he would not accompany them on this trip.

During the next two days, Abdul gathered everything he needed for the next trip. Food, drinks, suitable clothes and everything he needed. Abdul knew he had another adventure ahead of him. An adventure more dangerous than what he had experienced with Saleh when they crossed the border into Sudan. First he had to cross the desert, which was hot during the day and extremely cold at night. And then crossing the sea with its waves that have hit many migrant boats and sent them to the bottom.

Abdul did not tell his family in Eritrea about his next emigration. Rather, he told another lie to his mother, who was very saddened by the distance from her son and angry at her mother for taking her son to the border. He told her that he would be very busy in the coming days and that he could not call her. Abdul's mother wanted her son to be safe anywhere, anytime. She told him to call her again when he had a chance. And she advised him to stay away from problems of all kinds. The poor mother did not know that her son was embarking on another adventure. And she would be very surprised to hear his news from Libya. More than the first surprise when she heard his news from Sudan.

The big day had come when Abdul began his journey. Across the Sahara sands to Libya. And then across the sea to Italy. But he still had no money for the crossing of the sea. He intended to have his father pay the cost of crossing that sea. The father who had no idea of his son's crazy thoughts and actions.

# Chapter Five

# A Second Migration Across the Sahara Sands

Abdul came to the meeting point, which was on the outskirts of the Sudanese capital, Khartoum. He realized he wasn't the only one wanting to emigrate to Libya when he saw ten other people of different nationalities there. In addition to Abdul, there were ten other people who wanted to cross the desert to Libya. Most of these people came from Sudan. But there were also people of Eritrean descent, from Syria, Somalia and Bangladesh. Abdul gave the money and the phone to the smugglers as he had agreed with. He then joined the 10 others who got into the open Land Rover.

The car drove north towards the Libyan border. And after a drive that lasted almost five hours before it got dark, the car pulled up and everyone was told to get out. Abdul was nervous and didn't know what was going on. One of the smugglers pointed his hand and said:

"Do you see that hut? You're going to spend the night there tonight. And tomorrow morning our friends will bring another car and take you across the border. Now go to sleep because you have a long way ahead of you tomorrow."

Nobody had a choice except to obey the orders of this smuggler, who carried guns, like his friend. The smugglers got into their pickup and drove off. Abdul and the others went to the hut surrounded by a few trees in the midst of this nothingness and darkness. Abdul went to this hut with the others. Everyone was surprised when they found three people there. They were three teenagers who, like everyone else in this place, were forced to emigrate to Europe by the circumstances in their homeland. These three said that they had arrived at this place at noon that day. They were also told that they would be taken to the border the next morning. Abdul entered this hut and looked for a better place to sleep. The whole place was full of sand. Abdul lay down on the sandy ground like everyone else and prepared to sleep.

Now everyone started talking to each other about what they would do if they came to Europe. Three Sudanese were going to Libya to work and settle down. They had no interest in going to

Europe. Everyone was surprised by their words and asked them why Libya.

Libya was then a place of conflicts and wars. It was not a place to work and settle down. But everyone had their own goals and opinions.

"You, what country will you go to when you reach Europe?" one of those present asked Abdul.

"To Switzerland," Abdul replied. "I will go to Switzerland because all the offices of the United Nations and many other organizations are in Geneva. They know about human rights there."

"Switzerland is a country of banks, you know where the money is, yes? That's why you're going to Switzerland, isn't it?" someone interjected. Everyone laughed.

"No, not for money. I just want to be treated like a human being. And if I don't come to Switzerland, I'll go to another country, no matter where," Abdul replied.

Everyone who wanted to go to Europe had different destinations. Among them were those who wanted to go to Germany because they had relatives there. And some of them who wanted to go to Sweden and the Netherlands for different reasons.

After chatting and laughing in the midst of that nothingness, everyone went to sleep and waited for what was awaiting them tomorrow, the day they were supposed to cross the border into another country. There were no birds that could wake people up in this place. Everyone awoke to the bright sunlight streaming through the roof of the old hut. For everyone it was their last sleep in this country. Now everyone was waiting for a truck.

Several hours passed and no car came. Abdul began to wonder if a car was really coming to pick them up. Or did these smugglers take the money and go on their own way? And had they abandoned these fourteen people in this void to their fate?

Abdul, like everyone else there, was concerned. He walked left and right to see if a car was coming. Some were so worried that they were convinced no one would come to get them and they prepared to walk somewhere in one direction, maybe they could get lucky and reach a village. Tension and

*Anxious dreams kindle at the desert,*
*and people who are looking for a better life.*
*In the dim darkness they try to move,*
*looking for a peaceful life.*
*But it hasn't turned out that way yet.*
*Where it is difficult to gain the right of life.*

~ Chat GPT

fear filled everyone. Suddenly, Abdul, who was standing at some distance from the others, shouted, "There's a car coming. Look at the dust, they're coming."

Everyone ran to Abdul, overwhelmed with joy and relief. The car arrived with three smugglers that afternoon and took away some of the anxiety and stress that filled the place. The smugglers got out of the car and one of them asked if everyone was there. And he started counting the people. All were there. But if the car had come a few minutes later, not all the people would have been there. In their desperation they would have set out on their own way. Nobody dared to ask the smugglers why they were so late and why they hadn't come in the morning. They were armed like their friends before.

A smuggler ordered everyone to get their belongings together and get on the car. The car was an open Land Rover (pickup). The smugglers were known to use these types of cars to smuggle people and goods. Everyone started to get into the back of the car. Then Abdul asked one of the three smugglers:

"Is there an empty seat in the front?"

"No, princess, go with the others or we'll leave you here to die," the smuggler replied, pushing Abdul to the back of the car.
Abdul got into the back of the truck with the others.

"Be careful dealing with these people. They are evil. They care about nothing but the money they take from people like you and me. We must follow their orders," someone said in a low voice to Abdul.

The car with the 14 migrants and the three smugglers headed towards the Libyan border. It was a very long drive through the desert. And dust rose up around the car. The dust covered everyone in the back of the car so they couldn't see each other. After a long journey, night came and the car stopped. The smugglers said everyone would spend the night here. Abdul got some food out of his bag. But tiredness and exhaustion left him with no appetite. The sand was everyone's bed in the desert. And it was very cold there. During the day it was very hot. But at night it was almost as cold as if everything was frozen over. You didn't know if it was winter or summer in this desert, even though it was January.

Abdul was lying on the sand, using his bag as a pillow. He looked at the sky. Oh my god, the view of the sky was beautiful in the middle of this desert. The stars were shining everywhere and they were very close. Abdul kept looking at these stars meditating on them. How wonderful it felt to see something so beautiful in the midst of these circumstances. Abdul, who loved space and everything in it, thought long about this great scene. He hoped his future would brighten up like these stars when he reached Europe. Sleep overtook Abdul as he gazed at the stars. As soon as Abdul fell asleep, he woke up to the sound of gunshots. The shots were fired by one of the smugglers.

"Everyone wake up, we're moving," the smuggler shouted, firing in the air.
It was still night. Abdul looks at the watch in his hand and realizes it was five in the morning.

"Damn' these people, it's still night, why don't they let us sleep peacefully?" Abdul said to himself.

Abdul and the others got in the car and set off before sunrise. The car was going very fast and everyone was holding onto something on the car to keep from being thrown out. A scarf flew from one of the passengers, which he used to protect his face from the dust. When he tried to hold his scarf and lost his grip on the car, he flew like his scarf out of the car. What a scary scene that was for the others.

"Stop! Stop!" everyone on the back of the car yelled.

The car stopped and the smugglers came out angry.

"What's your problem?" asked the smugglers.

Abdul and the others told the smugglers that someone had fallen out of the car because of their extreme speed. Four people got out to look for the fallen person. They hardly saw him in the midst of these trenches until they heard a voice weeping and crying, "Help, help!". They came to this person and found that he could hardly stand. One of his legs was broken. The four helped the man reach the car and then one gave him a sedative for the severe pain he was suffering. It was lucky for this poor man that the ground was sand. Otherwise it might have been worse. Abdul and the others asked the smugglers not to drive at that speed. Because it was very dangerous for those who were in the back of the car. But the smugglers' response was harsh.

"We won't slow down, but increase our speed to reach our destination quickly. Everyone needs to hold on tight. Next time we might not stop if someone falls," said one of the smugglers.

The smugglers paid no attention to the poor young man who had been thrown off the back of the car like a piece of paper. They didn't even care about anyone's life. They didn't care at all. They were really bad people. That's why everyone had to hold on tight to not fall off this car. Perhaps they would be left in the middle of this miserable desert. The car continued to drive after this incident without slowing down. But accelerated more and more, as they had said.

After a while the car stopped. Everyone saw another car next to it. Another car that nobody could see before because of the desert dust. Abdul and the others were ordered to get out of the car. Then one of the smugglers came and told them:

"Our journey with you is finished. These are our Libyan friends. From here they will take care of you. They will drive you to Libya. Now everyone should take their luggage and get on this Libyan car," he added.

Abdul thought what a large network there was behind this smuggling business. People from different countries cooperate with each other in this illegal business.

Abdul took his bag and went to the Libyan car with the others. The car that was also driven by three smugglers. Except they were not Sudanese like before, but Libyans. They were also armed. For

Abdul, the scenes were like something out of a gangster movie. The two cars were going in opposite directions. The Sudanese returned towards Sudan, perhaps to tow other new migrants. And the other car that Abdul and the other migrants were in was heading into the Libyan territory.

The car stopped the next evening after another long journey. All would have to spend a second night in the desert. Abdul lay on the sand to be mesmerized by the sight of the sky again. A beautiful sight, just like last night. Abdul stared at the sky until he fell asleep as before.

What a big desert. Two days of non-stop driving a day and it's not over yet.

Everyone woke up on the new day, but not from the gunshots like last time. It was the screams of a smuggler screaming and saying, "Wake up you bastards, it's time to go."

Abdul, who was 15 years old, saw nothing good on this journey, only darkness. Darkness in which he could see the light of the stars and the beauty of the sky in the midst of this barren desert. Their third day was drawing to a close, and night was approaching. Everyone thought they were going to spend a third night en route. What a long journey! Night came and the car didn't stop. Abdul began to wonder why the car didn't stop. It usually stopped when night came so everyone could rest and sleep. He heard someone say, "Apparently there's no stopping tonight. Oh my god, it's going to be a long night." Everyone was very tired and wished the car would stop so they could sleep. But nobody dared to ask the smugglers to stop.

After a while, a few lights appeared at a distance. "Look, there are lights," they all said to each other. Everyone was happy to see lights on earth as the lights of the stars, even if they weren't as beautiful, but they were realistic and close. Now Abdul knew why the car hadn't stopped. Because the goal was near. The car continued towards these lights. The closer they got, the more numerous and larger the lights became. The car reached the lighted area, which was a small village in Libyan territory, after they had finally crossed the desert. The car continued to a building surrounded by farms. When the car stopped, Abdul and the other migrants were ordered to get out. The smugglers came and said that everyone would spend the night in this building called «Mazraa». And tomorrow would decide how to proceed. Abdul entered the building. It was full of migrants of different gender and nationalities. In the building there were many rooms full of people.

The smugglers used the rooms as a temporary prison for the migrants. For those who had not yet paid the money until their families paid them the required amounts. Abdul and the others entered one of these rooms. There were many other people in that room.

No one had any choice but to listen to the smugglers. There were many armed smugglers in this building running the «Mazraa». It was like a maximum-security prison. Nobody could escape from this prison. And nobody could sleep in the crowded room.

# Chapter Six

# **The Terrible Scene**

The new day began. The door of the room opened and Abdul and his group walked out. Except one person. This person hadn't paid the full amount, so he had to stay in that room until he would pay the rest of the amount. Abdul and the others made their way to a town called Sabha in central Libya, which was the agreed destination with the smugglers in Sudan. They got into another car with new smugglers and headed towards that destination. Abdul and the others left their companion, who had not paid the full amount, at that place and wished him good luck and salvation.

The car, this time with 13 immigrants, was moving towards the town of Sabha. After about 6 hours of driving, they came to an empty house in a small town. This house was apparently run by the smuggler network. Abdul entered this house hoping to have a better night than his previous nights. Everyone had run out of food, so they asked the smugglers to bring them food. The smugglers let Abdul and his companions into this house and told them that they would bring them food. Then they locked the door from the outside and left.

Abdul and the others kept waiting in this house for hours and they were very hungry. The smugglers who had said they would bring food didn't come. Everyone started looking for something to eat in this house. Some of them tried to break down the door to go out and look for something to eat. But all their attempts failed. The day passed and the night passed. For Abdul, who had wished for a better night, this was his worst night. Everyone was desperate and very hungry. They thought they would die in this miserable house.

On the next morning the smugglers came and brought food. Everyone was very angry with them. Because they were starving so badly and no one brought them something to eat. But they couldn't do anything. Abdul took the food from the smugglers and began distributing it to his comrades. Then he took his food because he was very hungry like the others. After everyone had regained their energy, they got back into the car as instructed. The car continued to move towards the town of Sabha.

Libya is a very big country. The distances between cities are huge. As a result of the conflicts and wars in the country at that time, drug and smuggling gangs controlled large areas in this country. There was no stable government.

After a long drive during the day, it was getting dark. The car stopped at another house, so the group had to spend the night on the road again. Abdul was afraid they would almost starve to death again. Luckily for them, the smugglers brought food this time and distributed it to Abdul and his fellow travellers. Everyone entered the house and this time no one worried about the door. One of the rooms in the house was completely stuffed with clothes. There were a lot of blankets there. Abdul and his companions lay down in this room. Abdul felt so good lying in those clothes. He couldn't resist sleep. Waking up from sleep in the morning, Abdul said to his comrades:

"I haven't slept like this since we moved from Sudan. What a restful night."

Everyone agreed and said it was the best night they had ever slept. In the afternoon two cars came, one empty and the other full of migrants. Abdul and his companions boarded the empty car driven by new smugglers. The smugglers said that all would arrive in the city of Sabha that day. This city that everyone longed for to get rid of their suffering.

The two cars continued their way and after hours reached the city, which is located in the center of Libya. At the point where they arrived there was a large camp full of immigrants. Everyone who came in those cars entered that camp. Abdul entered the camp and saw an army of migrants there. After a brief stay in this camp, they were called out. Then the smugglers started asking the newly arrived people one by one whether they wanted to stay in Libya or cross the sea to Italy.

Abdul did not know before how he would cross the sea and how he would meet smugglers who would help him cross the sea. But here it was these smugglers themselves asking people if anyone wanted to cross the sea. Abdul found that his problem of finding someone to help him cross the sea was solved. He replied to the smugglers that he wanted to cross the sea to Italy.

The smugglers then divided the people into two groups. A group that wanted to stay in Libya, like the three from Sudan who had come in the same car with Abdul, and another group that wanted to cross the sea and reach Europe. The smugglers ordered the group, who wanted to stay in Libya, to get into one of the cars parked there. They told them that they would take them to the center of this city. And they would be on their own there to mind their own business afterwards. Nobody knew what they really planned to do with them, whether they really drove them to the city center and left them to their own ways. Or did other things happen to them?

The other group, in which Abdul was and all who wanted to cross the sea, returned to the warehouse until further notice. Abdul went back to the big camp. The sun was just going down. Upon entering this warehouse, no one knew if it was day or night. Because darkness filled the place 24 hours a day.

Abdul first wondered if these smugglers could be trusted to help him cross the sea to Italy. Or were they deceitful people? But he saw no other choice. He'd come all the way across the desert by the same smuggling network. So he figured he might as well cross the sea with the same smugglers.

Abdul started talking to some people in the camp in the dark. They were people of different nationalities. Some of them said they were from Chad and Nigeria, and some were from Syria, Ethiopia, and many other countries. Most of these people wanted to cross the sea. And they had stayed in this camp for different periods of time. Some of them had been in the camp for two or three days. And others had been here for two or three weeks because they had not yet paid the money for their crossing of the desert. Oh my god, what they did to all the people who hadn't paid yet. Abdul wished that his family would quickly pay the cost of crossing the sea so that he would not remain in such a dark prison for a long time like those poor people.

The night passed, but nobody noticed. The next morning, Abdul and others were taken out by the smugglers to ask them for money to cross the sea. Abdul told them that his family would pay him the full amount required. Some of the other migrants had relatives in Europe who would bear the cost of the crossing. But Abdul had no one in Europe apart from his family at home. His family, who Abdul hoped would pay the money for their son quickly.

The smugglers told everyone who wanted to cross the sea that they would go to the capital, Tripoli, that day. They hoped that their families would actually pay the money. Otherwise, serious consequences threatened.

"You stay there in Tripoli until your families pay for your passage. And if they don't, believe me, you will regret your decision," one smuggler warned Abdul and the others.

That day the smugglers wanted to load four cars with immigrants. They had more than twenty people crammed into each car. It was unbelievable, more than 20 people in an open Toyota or Land Rover! The smugglers divided the migrants into four groups. They lined up each group behind a car. The smugglers went through these lines and took six to seven people from each line. The people who took them were slim and young. Among them was Abdul. Because he was a slim person in addition to his young age. The cars consisted of two cabins at the front. A cabin for the driver and another seat with him. And another cabin behind the driver, in which there were no seats. There was an empty space between the two doors.

The smugglers brought these slim little teenagers into this empty cabin. Abdul and six others went into the cabin in one of the cars. They were three girls and four boys, all teenagers. Seven people in such a small space. They could hardly breathe well. But, as usual, no one could refuse an order to these armed men. The rest of the migrants in the lines got into the back of the car. Everyone had to stay standing because there wasn't enough space otherwise. Abdul prayed to reach his goal in peace. And get rid of all those smugglers forever.

The three cars moved first. Then the car with Abdul in it followed them. The car was being driven by a 17-year-old boy. Children in Libya have not been spared from this dreadful smuggling either. After they left this city of Sabha, the car that Abdul was in, stopped. The young driver got out of his seat. Then he opened the door of the cab where Abdul and the other six were.

"I know you're upset here, so I've decided to give you a little exoneration," he told them.
Then he addressed his words to one of the three girls and said to her: "You, come with me to the front, there is an empty seat."

The poor girl was scared but went to the front with him. When the young driver returned to his seat, he pulled up a curtain that was between him and Abdul and the others, between the two cabins. Abdul wondered why the boy had pulled up the curtain. Is he going to do something that the others shouldn't see or what exactly? The car moved on again. After a short time, everyone behind the curtain could hear the driver addressing the girl and saying:

"Look, there are a lot of sweets here. Take what you want. I'll bring you food later, too."

Not everyone behind the curtain could understand what the boy was saying, except Abdul and another boy from Yemen. Not everyone understood the Arabic the driver spoke. The poor girl took some sweets.

"I want you to do something for me in exchange for what I'm giving you," the young driver said to the girl.

"What should I do?" the girl asked with a trembling voice.

"Don't worry, just a small thing," the boy replied.

"What?" the girl asked again.

"I want you to make me happy and suck my d*ck," said the young smuggler, undoing his pants. At that moment Abdul was shocked by what he heard and saw through the curtain. Everyone was shocked. Maybe not everyone understood what he was saying, but that scene through the curtain was enough to shock everyone. Abdul and the young Yemeni decided to intervene. They opened the curtain.

"What are you doing? Are you sick?" Abdul asked the young molester.

The driver got angry and stopped his car to get out with his gun. He pulled Abdul and the Yemeni out of the car. Everyone in the car was screaming. The driver pointed his gun in Abdul's face and said to him, "Did you call me sick?" Pointing his gun once at Abdul and once at the Yemeni, he said: "Do you know that I can kill you now and throw your corpse on this road? I am Libyan and this is my country. I do what I want to do."

"You are all just money to us. If it wasn't for the money you paid, I would have gotten rid of you a long time ago," he added, firing a few bullets into the air.

Everyone was appalled by the behavior of this psycho. After threatening and intimidating them, he told Abdul and the Yemeni man to get back in the car. He said if anyone dared interfere with what he was doing, he would shoot them with that gun. The mad driver got into his car and drove off at high speed to catch up with the other cars, with whom he communicated via walkie-talkie.

Abdul was very scared because this psycho had put the gun in his face. He thought maybe next time he'd do it and shoot. Abdul chose not to interfere with what the Psycho Driver was doing. When this psychopath caught up with his group, he again approached the girl to force her to do what he wanted. At first the girl tried to refuse. But after he threatened her with his gun, the poor girl had no choice but to cry and do as the psycho said. Everyone behind the curtain was deeply moved by this scene. Abdul didn't want to see or hear what was happening in front of him. He covered his head with the jacket he was wearing. The other two girls in the cabin were crying, shocked by what happened to their friend. What a horrible scene for these youngsters. A scene they would never forget. And the poor girl who was forced into terrible things at her young age! This moment would remain a nightmare in her entire life.

After this terrible incident, the car continued to drive as if nothing had happened. Who knows, maybe the driver had done it to another innocent girls before. Maybe it wasn't the first time he'd done something like this.

In the evening the convoy reached a small village near the capital Tripoli. All migrants got out of the four cars. The smugglers told them they would spend the night here in a large hall nearby.

And tomorrow everyone would be driven to the heart of the capital in small cars. The smugglers wanted to avoid suspicion by the police. So they wanted to put people in small, locked cars and take them around the capital.

Abdul and the others entered the hall, which was dark and very cold. Abdul couldn't sleep that night because of the cold in the hall. And because of the scenes he had seen that day. A scene that won't get out of his head for a long time.

# Chapter Seven

## The Capital Tripoli

After a long night everyone was waiting for it to be over. The next morning came and the smugglers brought five small cars to take the migrants to the capital. They again divided the people into four groups. The small cars were only fit for four to five people. They had to bring people to the capital in four different rounds. So they divided the people into four groups. Each lap they took a group in the five cars. As before, a group consisted of 20 to 22 people. The smugglers drove the first group in the five cars towards the capital, Tripoli. They left a gap of five to ten minutes between each car. And they told the drivers to take different routes to the destination. The destination was a house in the center of Tripoli. The smugglers wanted to bring all the migrants into this house. There they wanted to deal with them in the matter of crossing the sea.

The five cars got the first group to the goal and then came back to take over a second group that included Abdul. This group was composed of 21 people. Abdul got into one of the five cars along with three other migrants. The cars drove towards the capital. Abdul turned to see if there was a car behind them. But he saw nothing. Each car would take a different route when it reached the outskirts of the capital, in addition to the distances, they kept between each car. They did this to evade the police in Tripoli. Or what's left of it, that is.

Abdul reached the outskirts of Tripoli in the car. Bullet impacts were clearly visible on the buildings. And many buildings had collapsed completely. It was clear that Tripoli had seen bitter fighting between parties and militias since the start of the local revolution in 2011. The revolution that broke out against the regime of Colonel Muammar Gaddafi, who was then the ruler of the country. Then it turned into an armed conflict and a civil war that lasted for years and was not yet over. Abdul had heard there was an armed conflict in Libya before he came there. But he didn't expect it to get to the point where he saw entire cities destroyed and militias controlling the country. There was no prevailing law in Libya. It was survival of the fittest, as Charles Darwin said.

The car Abdul was in drove through the streets of Tripoli toward the destination. Suddenly they saw a police car chasing them. Everyone was scared when they saw the police. Abdul believed that if the police arrested them, they would all be sent back to their country. He was afraid to return to Eritrea. The country he had come all the way from to escape.

The driver told everyone to calm down and be normal. The police stopped the car. The policeman came and looked at everyone. Then he asked the driver for the documents. The policeman checked the documents and told the driver to follow the police car to the station.

"Is everything okay?" the driver asked the police officer.

"Follow me to the station and we'll see if everything's okay there," was the police officer's reaction.

Everyone was very tense. The driver followed the police car to the station as ordered. On the way to the station, the driver told Abdul and the others to say they worked at a nearby farm if the police asked them what they were doing there.

When they got to the police station, the officer told the group to get out of the car.

"Where are you from and what are you doing in Tripoli?" the policeman began to ask the group.

None of the four immigrants knew Arabic except Abdul.

"We are Sudanese and work on a farm on the outskirts of Tripoli," Abdul replied. "And we came to buy some things like food and clothes from here."

"Where are your documents?" the policeman asked.

"We left it at the farm, we didn't know we would need them here," Abdul replied.

"Are you also from Sudan?" the policeman asked the other three.

Abdul jumped in and said: "They do not speak Arabic. As you know, in Sudan we have many tribes and we have many different languages. But I assure you that they are from Sudan," Abdul replied, "If you wish, we can go back to this farm to see the documents, Mr. Officer, " he added.

The police officer approached the driver and told him that he had to pay a fine because his driver's license was no longer valid. The driver paid the fine. After that, the policeman said that everyone could go. Abdul and the others returned to the car. Their faces were filled with joy because they were not arrested. Maybe the policeman wasn't really interested in these people. Maybe he didn't want to waste his time with them. So he let them go without serious questioning or investigation.

The car left the police station premises. The driver was very impressed with what Abdul had done to the policeman. And the three migrants who were from Ethiopia also thanked Abdul for his behavior. After the car moved away from the police station, the driver started yelling at the Ethiopians and said:

"He saved you idiots! Why don't you speak Arabic in Ethiopia? Arabic is a big language. Your Ethiopian language will not help you if you leave your country."

The idiot driver didn't know that Abdul had saved him as well. The driver was so happy that he stopped at a shop. He bought there food for Abdul and the others. And he started addressing Abdul and said:

"Take the food, it's a gift from me because you did a good job at the police station."

Then he asked Abdul: "Why are you going to Italy? There is nothing the Italians can offer you. Did you know that the Italians were colonizers of Libya in the past? They have done nothing for us except destroyed our country and have plundered our wealth. I hate them."

"I want to go to Switzerland, not Italy," Abdul replied.

"They are all the same. They are all European bastards," the driver said.

"Here in Libya you can work with us. You work with us in smuggling. Believe me, you will make a lot of money in a very short time. You can live here, maybe get married later, raise a family, and live happily with them here," he added.

Little did he know that Abdul would have shot all the smugglers if he could. How should he work and live with them? Abdul hated these people very much. And his hatred increased after the innocent girl incident with the harassing driver. All smugglers brutalized people. They treated them like animals, not people.

Abdul told the driver that he had no intention of working and living in Libya. He told him he just wanted to go to Europe and start a new life there. The driver was disappointed with Abdul's answer. He wanted to lure him into their evil smuggling network. The driver told Abdul he would regret going to Europe and would not find such an opportunity there. Abdul ignored his words. He thought to himself that he would rather return to Eritrea than work with these smugglers. At least nobody there gets attacked as the smugglers do here.

The car had reached its destination: the house in the center of the capital, Tripoli. The house was surrounded on all sides by a concrete wall. The wall had an entrance that let the cars in from the front. The car pulled into the walled courtyard. Abdul saw a group of smugglers and brokers in the house. There were many rooms in this house. Rooms like the ones Abdul had seen the first day he entered Libya, at the place called «Mazraa».

After dropping Abdul and the others off, the driver went to get another group. The group of smugglers and brokers at that location took Abdul and the others and took them to one of the rooms. The smugglers used these rooms as cells within a prison. Every room was full of people. This time the smugglers in this place were not only Libyans. There were even Eritreans and Sudanese working with them. Who knows, maybe the smugglers had lured them in as the driver was trying to lure Abdul. These Eritrean and Sudanese smugglers were more ruthless in their dealings with migrants than the

Libyans. They beat them brutally. Abdul saw how they treated people.

"Damn' those people who treat their compatriots and others harder than the Libyans. They think they will impress the Libyans with their brutality. F*k them all," Abdul kept saying to himself.

Four smugglers entered the room where Abdul was. One came to Abdul.

"Do you speak Arabic?" asked the smuggler.

"Yes," replied Abdul.

"Take this phone and call your people. Tell them to pay your crossing money," the smuggler said.

"Ok, how much is required?" Abdul asked.

"Two thousand dollars," the smuggler replied.

"And what's the final price?" Abdul asked again.

"What do you think, I am selling you vegetables?" the smuggler said in an angry voice. "Now pick up the phone and tell your people to bring the two thousand dollars. Otherwise, they'll never see their son again."

Abdul picked up the phone and called his uncle who was in Qatar. His uncle had lived in

Qatar for a long time. Abdul did not call his family in Eritrea but his uncle in Qatar because the communication network in Eritrea was very weak. Especially with calls from Libya it was very difficult. Abdul wanted to communicate with his family through his uncle in Qatar. He had his phone number in his head. Connectivity from Qatar to Eritrea was much better compared to Libya. The uncle was surprised when he saw the Libyan phone number. The surprise was even greater when he heard his nephew's voice on that phone. Abdul explained the situation to his uncle. And asked him to tell his family that their son was detained in Libya, waiting for him to cross the sea. They should pay the sum of two thousand dollars as soon as possible. The uncle was concerned and angry at his nephew's reckless behavior. He asked Abdul why he did that and why he hadn't told anyone before he went to Libya. The smuggler snatched the phone from Abdul's ear as he spoke. He urged the uncle to transfer the money in full and quickly if he didn't want anything bad to happen to his nephew. Then he turned off his phone. This move was part of the blackmail and threats used by smugglers on all migrants. After that, the smuggler said to Abdul, "You should pray that your family will respond quickly, otherwise we will sell your organs one by one," and walked away.

Abdul wished that his uncle would take the message to his family. And his family had to pay the money quickly. The uncle had no choice but to break the news to Abdul's family.

The first day passed. Abdul thought all day about what his family would do. He couldn't sleep at night. He had too much to think about.

There were many people in the room Abdul was in. Some of them said they spent a week in these cells. And others said they had been here more than a month because they had not yet paid for their passage across the sea. Abdul was very afraid that he would end up like these poor people and spend many weeks in this hell.

At noon the next day, a smuggler entered the room and shouted, "Abdul, who is Abdul?" Abdul came to the smuggler. He got him out of the room. The smuggler told Abdul after taking him out of the room that a person named Osman called and asked for him.

"He is my uncle, he wanted to talk to me about my family and the amount you guys are asking for," Abdul said.

"Now take this phone and call him back," said the smuggler.

Abdul picked up the phone and called his uncle Osman. Osman replied and told him that he had spoken to his family. He told him that his family, especially his mother, were very worried about him. Abdul asked him if his family would send the money so he could cross the sea or what.

"Listen, Abdul, your family agreed to pay the amount because you left them no choice with your reckless behavior. But as you know, Eritrea is a very closed country. It will take a very long time for the money from Eritrea to get into the hands of these smugglers. And you can make these people angry if you pay the money late. They will hurt you. We don't want anything to happen to you," was the uncle's reply.

"Please uncle, tell me there is another solution!" Abdul asked his uncle.

"I told your family that I will pay the money now. Because it is much easier to send it from Qatar. Your parents will give me the money later. The most important thing now is how we get you out of this situation," the uncle explained his solution. "Now give the smuggler the phone so he can tell me where to transfer the money to." Abdul gave the phone to the smuggler. He was very happy to hear the news from his uncle. Abdul thought he would finally be rid of this hell.

Eritrea did not have advanced means of transferring money. The only option was to send the amount with someone you know. But this method took too long. In addition, Abdul's family did not know anyone who could bring the money to Libya. Osman agreed with Abdul's family that he would transfer the money. And he looked at the bill with them later. This was the best solution they found. Abdul's uncle spoke to the smuggler. The smuggler told him to transfer the money to an account in Tripoli.

The smuggler arranged with Osman to transfer the money within the next two days. Abdul returned to the room. His face was filled with joy. Because he would be leaving this awful place soon.

In the room there was a bathroom. It was used by the prisoners to relieve themselves and take a shower at the same time. A foul stench came from that place. A smell that no one in this room could escape. Abdul avoided entering the bathroom unless absolutely necessary. He never intended to shower there. So that was another reason why he wanted to leave this place.

The second day passed, and Abdul counted every second of it. On the third day, Osman transferred the amount agreed with the smuggler. That day, Osman spoke to Abdul again. He told him that his mother could neither eat nor sleep because she was very worried about her son. Abdul's mother, who always heard that many were not lucky and did not cross the sea. Rather, they sank to the bottom and became food for the fish. She was so afraid of losing her son in that sea. Abdul deeply regretted this news about his mother. He always said he felt sorry for his mother for no reason. But he hoped that with her prayers she could overcome all this suffering. He wanted her to hear very good news soon when he was safely across the sea.

The smugglers had received the $2,000. They said to Abdul that he would leave here soon. Abdul really wanted to leave this prison and cross the sea to Europe. But sometimes things don't go our way. In Tripoli, after a period of calm, a bitter fight broke out between the militias. The smugglers said they were currently unable to take anyone out of the rooms because of these fights. They were worried about their safety and their businesses. Not about the migrants.

At first Abdul was very upset about this news because he had to stay longer in this stinking room and with these smugglers who only wanted money. But he realized that it would not be safe for him to go out in the middle of a war. It could be more dangerous for his life than this prison.

The people heard gunshots and cannons in this place day and night. There was a big war in the inner city. It erupted between groups that neither Abdul nor anyone else in this prison knew. Nobody knew how long this fight would last and when it would be quiet again. Abdul wanted to make his mother happy soon. He wished it would all be over quickly.

A week passed and the fight still did not calm down. A week passed and Abdul counted the seconds every day. Everyone who had paid to cross the sea was very upset there. They resented the prison, where they were served one meal a day. The same food every day. The meal consisted of pasta and tomato sauce. Every day the smugglers took three or four people from the prison to cook these noodles. One meal a day made anyone who got here fat thin. And everyone who was thin like Abdul got thinner. Abdul had been eating these noodles every day for more than a week. And only once a day. But that wasn't his biggest concern. Rather, his biggest concern was to cross the sea to Europe. Europe which he considered a paradise to fulfill his dreams.

Another week had passed and the battle for Tripoli was not over. Some of the people in the room with Abdul were crazy and they were screaming. They even wanted to get out of prison in the middle of the fight. But the cruelty and brutal beatings of the smugglers left no choice but to remain silent. Abdul saw no choice but to pray and be patient and wait for relief. Everyone got worse every day. Those who were not mentally strong deteriorated. Some people became ill from severe mental illness. And some of them despaired.

After 18 days, the war gradually began to subside. Abdul no longer heard the sounds of the heavy weapons. But he could intermittently hear gunshots. Finally, he felt a glimmer of hope to leave this place. Two days later the war stopped completely. Nobody heard more shots. Now all the migrants started demanding to go to sea as soon as possible before a new war began.

# Chapter Eight

# On the Boat Full of Water

The smugglers wanted to get rid of those who had paid the money because the rooms were crowded with people. The next evening three small cars came to take Abdul and the others to the sea. The smugglers put four people in each car and drove to a small village near the sea. This village was near a city called Misrata. The cars took Abdul and the others to new a housing in this village. This time there weren't many people in this big warehouse. There were only four people. The camp was guarded by one person. The guard always locked the camp from the outside.

The guard came to Abdul and the others and told them that the police are very strict on the sea these days. So everyone had to wait until the police had gone.

Abdul thought he was unlucky. He said to himself: "I got rid of Tripoli after more than three weeks and now I have to wait in this place again when I'm so close to the sea, what an unlucky person I am." He thought his fate was punishing him. But he forced himself to have faith. He now had but one step to reach the coast of Italy. A step, but big enough to decide his fate. Crossing the Mediterranean Sea. One step and he made his mother either happy or sad forever. Now he could only wait in this camp and be optimistic.

On the evening of the second day, a new car came with four girls. The girls had signs of horror on their faces. The guard led them into the camp. Abdul approached them and asked them:

"Are you okay? "

"There's nothing okay here.", one of the girls replied.

Like Abdul, the girls were from Eritrea. Their ages were between 17 and 19 years. Abdul started talking to these girls a little.

"What happened to you?" he asked.

"We came to Libya to go to Italy. Just like you. But we were unlucky and were kidnapped by the Islamic State on our way to Tripoli. Then they took us to one of the places they control. We were with them for more than four months," one of them replied.

"Oh my god, what did this ISIS do to you then?" asked Abdul.

"They let us cook and do their laundry for them. And other bad things. They made life difficult for us. We suffered from them," the girl said.

"I'm really sorry to hear that. But how did you get away from them?" Abdul asked again.

"Eventually we found a way to escape when the government attacked them and we fled from there," said another girl.

"And how did you end up here?" Abdul wanted to know.

"After we fled from ISIS, we came to a town called Misrata. We looked for brokers there who could help us to enter Europe. There we found an Eritrean. We told him we wanted to cross the sea to Europe. And our families would pay for us. This Eritrean contacted some smugglers and then they took us by car to bring us here," said one of the girls. "What a story! You haven't paid for the sea fare yet, have you?" asked Abdul.

"No, not yet. But we've talked to our relatives in Europe, they'll pay for us soon," answered one.

The poor girls in Libya had suffered a lot from the Islamic State. At that time, IS was widespread in Libya and controlled many areas there.

Abdul wasn't done asking the girls. While he was talking with the girls, the camp guard suddenly entered and said:

"To all who want to cross the sea. Get ready. You will move now."

Abdul wanted to continue his conversation with the girls, but he had to go now. He had waited a long time for this moment. He had to leave before the police showed up again. Abdul wished the girls all the best and good luck on their journey.

"Maybe we'll meet in Italy," he said to them, and everyone smiled.

Everyone went to the sea, leaving the four girls in the camp. It was around 1:00 a.m. when a car picked up Abdul and others to take them to the sea. Abdul came to the sea and found many people standing in front of a boat. He was ordered to stand in line with the people in front of the dinghy. There were many armed smugglers on site. They ordered all migrants to get on this boat. Some migrants refused to get on the inflatable boat. They feared the boat would sink and everyone would drown. But the smugglers forced everyone into the boat and threatened to kill with their guns anyone who refused. Abdul had no choice but to get on that inflatable boat and put his trust in God.

The boat was medium-sized and had about 40 people on board. One of the smugglers gave the boatman, who was also a migrant, a compass, and told him to take the north-west direction with the compass.

The boat left in the dead of darkness. Everyone on board was praying that they would reach the coast of Italy safely. The boat moved away from land until land was no longer in sight. After hours of sailing in complete darkness,

*The little stone sinks into the deep sea,*
*Screaming noises make us feel sad,*
*Deep waves and intense noise all around us,*
*And we try to cross the sea by smuggling,*
*We're trying to cross the sea with secret steps.*
*And our dreams are filled with dangers in smuggling,*
*We're trying to get out of this deep sea.*
*We're trying to flee to freedom,*
*But the path is neither simple nor easy,*
*But we still try to cross the sea by smuggling.*

~ Chat GPT

the sun began to rise. Abdul turned left and right and saw only the blue sea. The boat was so full of people that some of them sat on top of each other.

The boat drifted northwest for hours at sea. Nobody saw any land yet. After a while, water started seeping into the boat from below. Everyone was startled to see water right under their feet. More and more water seeped into the boat. Everyone thought the end was near. Some of them screamed and cried in desperation and even urinated on their clothes. And some of them recited their prayers believing that the end had not yet come.

In the boat were men, women and children. Children who had seen nothing good in this world. Except suffering with their parents. As many despaired, a large ship appeared in the distance. Everyone who saw the ship shouted: "Look, there is a ship, it will save us!"

As this gigantic ship approached, the boat was flooded with water. The ship was approaching, and everyone was calling for help.

"Help!" everyone on the boat yelled.

The ship approached the boat and threw a ladder at the migrants, who were now fully in the water. They began climbing the ladder to the ship one by one until everyone was rescued from the sinking boat. Luckily no child, woman or man drowned in that sea.

The ship was a merchant ship full of containers. Luckily for them, it got there just in time. If the ship hadn't been perfectly timed, everyone would have drowned at the sea. Abdul along with the others thanked the ship's crew for helping them escape the inevitable sinking. He was very happy not to die in that dinghy and become food for the fish. He saw the boat with his own eyes as it sank shortly after they were rescued from the boat. Abdul thought of his mother, who was very worried about him. He wished that she would hear very good news from her son soon.

Abdul now waited for the support ship, which contacted the merchant ship's crew. The support ship belonged to a non-governmental organization. After about an hour the ship came. Abdul and everyone else were brought onto this support ship. Then they were completely searched there. After that they were given snacks as everyone was starving.

The ship made its way to the Italian island of Lampedusa. Abdul wanted to sleep on the ship, but he couldn't because it was too cold. But he was so happy because he believed his dreams could come true soon. The ship sailed until night came. And sailed all the night. Having travelled all this distance, Abdul wondered how they were supposed to have travelled all this distance in the inflatable boat. He knew that if the merchant ship hadn't saved them, everyone on the boat would have been gone forever.

# Chapter Nine

# **Welcome to Italy**

The relief ship arrived at the Italian island of Lampedusa early in the morning. All migrants were dropped off there to be searched again by the police. After the search, they were taken by bus to a large refugee camp on the island. The officers took Abdul's fingerprints. After that, a staff member gave him some clothes and took Abdul to show him his room. The rooms were large and there were more than twelve beds in one room. Abdul, who hadn't slept for the past two days, lay in a bed and slept like he hadn't slept in over a month. In the evening he woke up to go to dinner like everyone else. He waited his turn to be served dinner. He ate his dinner and went back to bed to sleep again.

Abdul had not seen a bed during his stay in Libya. Rather, once he slept on the sands of the desert, and once he spread out his clothes to sleep. He was relieved to find a bed here. He tried to catch up on sleep. Or at least part of it.

The next morning, an employee came to Abdul and asked him to accompany him to the office. Abdul went to the office with this employee. A woman and another staff member were sitting in the office. The woman asked Abdul for the reason for his trip to Italy and his personal details. Abdul told them that he came to Europe in search of security and a future. And to avoid persecution in his home country.

"19 years," answered Abdul, who had a good command of English.

Abdul believed that if he declared his age over 18, he would be free to go anywhere he wanted. And that minors under the age of 18 would always be monitored or locked up in a house or camp. He thought minors couldn't move as they wanted. So he lied and told the woman that he was 19 years old. Everyone in the office was surprised and told him he couldn't be 19. Abdul initially insisted that he was 19 years old. But when nobody believed him and they forced him to tell his real age, he confessed and told them the truth that he was just 15 years old.

Abdul finished his interview with the woman after telling her everything she wanted to know. As he left the office, one of the employees gave him a phone card and told him that he could use this card to call his family and reassure them that he was fine. The phone card was loaded with five euros credit. Abdul couldn't believe it. He was so excited that he could finally call his mother. He took the card and ran to the phone booth.

He tried to call his mother in Eritrea. But it did not work. He tried several times, but all attempts failed. The Eritrean network was very bad. Finally, he decided to call his uncle in Qatar. The uncle was very happy when he heard Abdul's voice again. Abdul told him that he had arrived safely in Italy. He told him that he could not speak to his mother in Eritrea. So he asked his uncle to assure his mother that her son had crossed the sea without any problems.

Abdul didn't want his family to know about the dangers he was facing. He told his family that everything was fine every time they asked him.

"Do you know how worried your mother is about you? It's indescribable," said the uncle to Abdul.

Abdul asked his uncle to call his mother and calm her down as soon as possible.

"Tell her that her son will call her if he finds the opportunity soon. I want to hear her voice and she certainly wants to hear mine," Abdul sent his message to his mother through the uncle.

He knew that the uncle would calm his sister down. But he wanted to talk to his mother himself if he got the chance.

After reassuring his family, Abdul wanted now to get out of the camp and go for a walk on the island. But he could not leave this camp. The camp was surrounded on all sides with fences and wires. In addition to the police officers who were on duty everywhere, there were many surveillance cameras. Abdul tried to find a way out, but he couldn't. He said to himself it's okay and walked around the camp. He met a few people in the camp who used to talk to them to relieve himself a little.

In the evening Abdul received new information. Tomorrow he would go to Sicily with others. Then he rejoiced that he would get away from this camp and this isolated island. The island of Lampedusa was far removed from the rest of Italy.

He was going to Sicily by sea. But he felt safe because this time he wasn't going in a rubber dinghy, but in a safe ship.

On the third day, Abdul and others were taken by car to the island's port. There they boarded a large ship with the police. Then the ship headed for Sicily.

Abdul enjoyed the time with the view of the sea and the islands. He felt safe. He was beginning to taste a little of the security he had been looking for so long. But he was remembering the people he left behind in Libya. Like the four girls who suffered under ISIS. And the poor girl molested by the car driver on the way to Tripoli. He wished they could all get out of the hell in Libya. And had a future where they could start a new life. A life in which they remembered everything they went through to reach their goal.

Abdul arrived in Sicily by ship that evening. Then they were taken to another refugee camp by buses that were waiting for them there. The camp was in a small village in Sicily. When Abdul came to this camp, he was served dinner there. Then an employee told him that his bed number 18 was in hall seven. Abdul came into the hall and saw many beds stacked on top of each other. He climbed onto bed number 18, which was above another bed.

Now, lying on this bed, he began to think how he could get out of the camp and begin his journey to Switzerland. Switzerland, that was Abdul's last destination. Finally, he decided that the following day he had to inspect the village and look for a way out of the camp.

The next day, Abdul found that this camp was not closed and had no wall at all. Everyone was free to go out and walk through the village. Abdul found his biggest problem had been solved. Now, he just had to look for a means of transport to the north of Italy. Abdul was good at geography and knew where to go first to get to Switzerland. That's why he decided to go first to Rome and then to Milan. And from Milan to his final destination Switzerland.

Abdul went to the center of the village to look for a way to reach Rome. After a long search, one of the Italians told him that from here he first had to go to another village and from there he could find a bus to Rome. And he told him that there was only one bus that went from here to the other village early in the morning every day. Now after he knew the bus schedule, he decided to start his onward journey to Switzerland on the next morning.

Abdul had 100 dollars in cash. He had brought it from Sudan and hid it in his clothes. He knew that there came a situation when he would need the money. But first he had to exchange the dollars for euros. He started asking the people in the camp if they knew anyone who could change dollars into euros. Finally, he found someone who could trade. But this person told Abdul that he could only give him eighty euros for the hundred dollars, which Abdul initially refused. But he didn't want to miss the bus the next morning. So, he accepted the offer and exchanged the hundred dollars for eighty euros.

Abdul awoke from his sleep the next morning before the sun came out. He left the camp and went to the bus stop. When the bus came, Abdul asked the driver if he could take him without paying. But the driver refused and told Abdul to pay or he would not be able to take him on that bus. Abdul wanted to save the 80 euros to bring them to Switzerland. But it did not work. He bought his ticket and took the bus to the other village, which was not far away. Upon his arrival in the new village, he went in search of the bus that went to the capital, Rome. He found a ticket shop and bought his ticket to Rome. The ticket shop clerk told him that the bus would leave here at 5 p.m.

Abdul spent most of the day in front of the bus stop. He walked in the village, enjoying the beautiful views and talking to the friendly people. Cafes lined the streets of this village. But Abdul didn't want to spend whatever money he had unless it was necessary. He wanted to enjoy an Italian coffee, but he had a bigger goal than just a coffee.

The time for the bus came, Abdul got on the bus and the bus left. After a whole night, the bus arrived in Rome in the morning. Now Abdul wanted to take the train from Rome to Milan. But he felt that the train ticket was very expensive. He didn't have enough money for that ticket. So he went back to the bus station to catch another bus to Milan. He bought a ticket with his last change and took the bus in the morning to reach Milan in the evening.

Abdul didn't know what he would do after he arrived in Milan. He ran out of money. He hadn't got a cent. After all he decided to go to the train station in Milan hoping to find a way to go to Switzerland by train. He got to the station, but all his attempts to board a train failed. At the entrances, staff checked the tickets of each passenger when they wanted to enter the platforms. And Abdul didn't have any ticket. That's why he wasn't allowed to step on the platforms.

He kept walking around the station for more than an hour hoping to find a solution. He was sitting on a bench in the station when two people approached him. A man and a woman. They both wore red T-shirts that said "City Angels." The two asked Abdul what he was doing here and if they could help him. Abdul didn't hesitate to tell them the truth. He told them he wanted to take the train to Switzerland, but he had no money for the ticket. The woman told him that she worked for an organization that helps people and they could only offer him a bed to sleep in and some food. Abdul said that was all he needed for now until he found another solution.

He accompanied the two persons to the shelter. He went with them and they made a bed for him in the middle of a big hall full of people. Before leaving, they told him that two weeks was the maximum length of stay allowed in that place. And the food was only served at certain times. So he had to be present at meals, otherwise there was no food. He was very grateful to these two people. He thought that in these two weeks he would find a solution to come to Switzerland.

The days passed and Abdul still didn't find any solution. A week passed and left only one week for his stay at that place. One day a new boy came to the same shelter, also from Eritrea. This boy wanted to go to his brother in Germany. But like Abdul, he too had run out of money. He did not have the amount for a ticket to Germany. Abdul met him and they started exchanging discussions and walking around the city together. The boy, whose name was Biniam, told Abdul that his brother, who lived in Germany, would send him money to come to him.

"If my brother sends me enough money, I'll pay you for your ticket to Switzerland," Biniam said to Abdul.

Abdul felt hope thanks to Biniam and waited for the brother to send the money. Four days passed and on the fifth day Biniam received the money from his brother. He came to Abdul, gave him 20 euros and wished him well on his journey. Abdul didn't know how to thank this friend. He also wished him well and hoped that he could reach his brother without any problems.

The next morning, Abdul went to the train station and bought his ticket. He finally boarded the train headed to the country where he saw an opportunity to pursue his dreams. In the direction of Switzerland.

# Chapter Ten

# Did Abdul Find his Future?

Abdul arrived by train in a Swiss town called Bellinzona. There he sought the police to apply for asylum in that country. After he found police officers, they took him to their headquarters, where they searched him and then took him to a refugee camp in another place called Chiasso. An interview was conducted with him there in which he was asked about the reason for his coming into Switzerland and his personal data.

After spending two days in that camp, which was surrounded by wires and full of surveillance cameras and security guards, Abdul was transferred to another location in a small village because he was a minor. This new place was an underground bomb shelter. Above it was a football field. Most of the immigrants in this shelter were minors. But there were also children with their parents.

About one week later in the bomb shelter, the supervisors gave Abdul a train ticket and a map with an address and told him to go to Bern. Abdul took the ticket and the map and took the train to the city of Bern. He arrived in Bern and went to the address on the map. From there, someone took him by car to new accommodation in another village which was about an hour from Bern.

The new accommodation was next to a sports center. This is where Abdul went to school again after a long time. This school taught the German language. Abdul felt very good when he started to go to school again. He was very fond of studying. The last time he had gone to school was in Eritrea more than two years ago. In addition to school, he played sports in the nearby center. He felt that his life was gradually changing.

Abdul shared his room at the shelter with three other teenagers. Now he was trying everything to learn the language. He felt that learning the language would open many doors for him. Everything would be easy for him. So his focus on language was very big.

After four and a half months in this accommodation, he was transferred to a shared apartment, in a four-room house with six teenagers. Abdul joined them. Despite their different cultures and nationalities, they all treated each other with great understanding.

He had not yet completed a year in Switzerland and began attending high school. But he left after half a year because the language was a big challenge for him. He decided to go into the tenth grade and then to learn a suitable trade.

Abdul had made a big step forward by the time he entered tenth grade. A step that would change the course of many events in his life. He moved in with a Swiss family. Abdul had met the man of this family in high school. He was a teacher there. Abdul moved in with this man, John* (*name changed), and his partner Lisa* (*name changed). He got his first room od his own with this family. Abdul faced many challenges in Switzerland. The biggest of these challenges was the language. But he saw the chance that with this family he could learn and master the language much faster.

In fact, Abdul quickly learned the language with this family. John was a German teacher. So he was able to support Abdul a lot. Abdul not only learned the language with this family, but he was also able to get to know the laws and norms of the country. As well as their culture. He also got to know the other family members and relatives. With them he undertook many activities such as cycling and participating in many cultural programs. All these activities helped him to integrate better. The activities also helped him recover from the nightmares he was having. Yes, he had constant nightmares about Libya when he came to Switzerland. But now with the family, Abdul's life gradually improved. He was trying to start a new chapter in his life. A new page of forgetting all the tragedies he had been through.

In fact, Abdul was able to start a new page when he started learning a new trade. He was able to complete his vocational education after three years. And of course, John and his partner Lisa were always there to support him with whatever he needed.

Abdul lived with John and Lisa for four years. Four years were enough for Abdul to master the language and integrate very well in the country. After completing his education, he began to work, relying on himself for everything. Abdul left the hospitable family and began to live in his own apartment.

Abdul didn't forget what he had been through. He was trying to help many people who came to Switzerland like him. So they could face their challenges and reach their goals as he had done.

Life in Switzerland was not easy for Abdul at first. Everything was new to him. New culture, new laws, and new language. All of these were big challenges he faced. But because of his great determination and the support of everyone around him, he was able to overcome all these challenges. And he began to realize his dreams bit by bit. And with that, Switzerland was, as Abdul had hoped, a place where he could pursue his dreams and achieve his goals with pride.

# Thanks!

Thank you, Switzerland, for all the opportunities you gave me. I know that I have achieved my goals primarily through my effort and work. But thank you for being the right environment to achieve these goals. Thank you, Switzerland, for being an arena to make my dreams come true. Thank you for giving me freedom and security that I could not find in my own country. I would also like to thank my second family. John and Lisa. And all members of the family. Thank you for your unconditional support for me. With your support I was able to overcome many challenges and difficulties. Thank you to everyone who has supported and helped me in this life to reach my goals. And thank you, dear reader, for your interest in my story.